The World of Computer Vision

CHINAR DESHPANDE

For all the readers out there, who wish to make a change in the world

Contents

CONTENTS

1. Introduction

The 20th and 21st centuries have witnessed an unprecedented rise in the research, invention, and application of computing devices, enabling the human race to perform technical experiments and execute tasks at an incredible pace. With the expansion of the internet and digital tools for research, analysis, and communication, the concept of *Computer Vision* has begun to realize its full potential.

At its core, Computer Vision is an interdisciplinary field that focuses on automating the extraction of useful data from images and videos. Its primary objective is to replicate the tasks of the human visual system. From a scientific perspective, Computer Vision is concerned with theories allowing artificial systems to extract information from visual data, including video sequences, views from multiple cameras, or multi-dimensional data from medical scanners. Ideally, it aims to automate all tasks that any human visual system can take on.

The Evolution of Computer Vision

About seven decades ago, universities pioneering artificial intelligence began to explore the concept of Computer Vision. A general description that emerged revolved around Computer Vision as a field of Artificial

Intelligence that enabled computers and systems to derive meaningful information from digital images, videos, and other visual inputs, and to take actions or make recommendations based on that information.

However, this technical description doesn't capture the relevance of computer vision for a layman until it's contextualized in their everyday lives. As AI enables computers to "think," Computer Vision enables them to "see," observe, and understand. In this way, Computer Vision is one of the most compelling types of AI we encounter in our daily routines.

Understanding the Human Vision System

Many agree that Computer Vision helps us understand the complex human vision system and trains computer systems to interpret and gain a high-level understanding of digital images or videos. Developing a machine system with human-like intelligence was merely a dream in the early 1900s. Still, with the advancements in AI and Machine Learning (ML), such intelligent systems can now "see" and interpret the world around them similarly to human eyes and brains.

"The fiction of yesterday has become the fact of today."

Key Concepts in Computer Vision

Computer Vision, thus is a subfield of AI that trains computers to capture and interpret information from image and video data. Before diving deeper, let's define AI.

What is AI?

Artificial Intelligence (AI) refers to the simulation of human intelligence processes by computer systems. "Artificial" signifies that it is created by humans, while "intelligence" refers to a capability traditionally associated with humans. In essence, AI is the initial representation of one system's functionality through another.

It's an iterative process, with simulation being the initial representation of the functioning of a system. The vast all-encompassing nature of the internet allows AI to take information from computers all over the world, and as millions post information online, AI collects and disseminates the same to millions of others.

When browsing the internet, AI helps us choose the most appropriate website for our research needs. Computer Vision works similarly, utilizing information from various sources to provide the best results for user queries in seconds. For example, if an employee is assigned to write about a topic they know nothing about, their research could take hours or even days. In contrast,

AI could accomplish this task in seconds with more efficiency.

The State of Computer Vision Today

Modern programming languages have advanced significantly, allowing even those without a coding background to engage with Computer Vision and AI tools, provided they have the logical skills to apply them correctly. This democratization of technology has led to what some call "Prompt Engineering." However, the market for unqualified programmers is limited and requires convincing employers of their value.

Contextual Understanding and Applications

Understanding visual images involves transforming them into sensible descriptions that the real world can interpret, which could then lead to appropriate actions. This understanding is achieved by separating symbolic information from image-based data using models that incorporate geometry, physics, statistics, and learning theory.

Image data comes in many forms, such as video sequences, multi-camera views, multi-dimensional data from 3D scanners, 3D point clouds from LiDAR sensors, or medical scanning devices. Computer Vision encompasses various sub-domains, including scene reconstruction, object detection, event detection, video tracking, object recognition, 3D pose estimation, and more.

Computer Vision is a field rich with potential for academic research, with enough depth to generate comprehensive Ph.D. theses. This chapter is intended to ignite curiosity and encourage further exploration into the subject.

Computer Vision represents a powerful intersection of AI and human visual cognition, enabling machines to understand and interpret the visual world around them. As the technology continues to advance, its applications will only become more widespread, revolutionizing industries and everyday life.

Reference Links:

https://en.wikipedia.org/wiki/Computer_vision

https://www.ibm.com/topics/computer-vision

https://towardsdatascience.com/everything-you-ever-wanted-to-know-about-computer-vision-heres-a-look-why-it-s-so-awesome-e8a58dfb641e?gi=304d33b67357

2. Introduction to Image Formation

"Mirror, Mirror on the wall. Who is the fairest of them all?"

The mirror never lies, revealing the true image of a person. Have you ever wondered how an image is formed and observed by our eyes and processed by our brains?

Image formation is a fundamental concept in both human vision and computer vision, involving the projection of three-dimensional (3D) scenes onto two-dimensional (2D) image planes. This chapter delves into the science behind how images are formed, both geometrically and optically.

Image formation dates back to 1873 when German physicist Ernst Abbe laid the groundwork for understanding how microscopes form images. This chapter explores how light, material properties and sensor capture characteristics contribute to creating the images we see and interact with.

Factors Influencing Image Formation

Several factors affect how images are formed, including:

1. **Light Strength and Direction:** The intensity and angle of light emitted from the source influence how an object is illuminated and perceived.

2. **Material and Surface Geometry:** The texture, color, and shape of an object's surface, along with nearby surfaces, can impact how light is reflected or absorbed.

3. **Sensor Capture Properties:** The characteristics of the sensor or camera capturing the image, such as resolution and sensitivity, also play a significant role.

Real vs. Virtual Images

Images can be classified into two types: real and virtual.

1. **Real Images:** Formed by the actual intersection of light rays. These images can be projected onto a screen, like those produced by a projector.

2. **Virtual Images:** Formed when light rays appear to diverge from a point, creating an image that

cannot be projected but can be seen by the human eye.

Types of Images

There are four primary types of images to consider:

1. Binary Images: The simplest form, consisting of only two values—black and white (0 and 1). These are referred to as 1-bit images because each pixel is represented by a single binary digit.

2. Grayscale Images: Contain varying shades of gray, ranging from black to white.

3. Color Images: Utilize combinations of red, green, and blue (RGB) values to represent a wide spectrum of colors.

4. Multispectral Images: Capture data at different wavelengths across the electromagnetic spectrum, often used in remote sensing and medical imaging.

The Image Formation Process

The process of image formation involves two main components:

1. Geometric Image Formation: Determines where in the image plane the projection of a point in the 3D scene will be located.

2. Physics of Light: Determines the brightness of a point in the image plane based on illumination and surface properties.

Understanding Digital Images

A digital image represents visual objects, their characteristics, interior structure, and physical view. Digital imaging generally includes processing, compression, storage, and display of objects, with the added advantage of allowing as many copies of the original image as needed without sacrificing quality.

Two main components of digital images are pixel and resolution. Pixel is the smallest element of a digital image that can be manipulated through software. A pixel can be compared to an atom, where each is insignificant on its own, but together, they create stunning images. On the other hand, resolution refers to the total number of pixels in a digital image. Screen resolution, for instance, specifies how many pixels can be displayed horizontally and vertically on a screen (e.g., 1920x1080 for Full HD). So, a screen with a resolution of 1920x1080 -- 1080p or full HD -- can display 1,920 pixels horizontally and 1,080 pixels vertically. Typical recording densities for personal computer monitors (PCs) include 640 (horizontal) by 480 (vertical, standard VGA), 800 by 600, and 1024 by 768 (SVGA).

Fun Fact: A group of 1 million pixels is called a 'megapixel'. A lot of phones and cameras have different resolution sizes, so the higher the megapixels, the better the quality of the photo.

If pixels are atoms, then similar to protons, neutrons, and electrons making up an atom, "subpixels" make up a pixel. Patented in 1938, the theory of Red, Green, and Blue subpixels posits and proved that any color could be represented in these shades if the values ranged from 0 to 255. Each of the red, green, and blue subpixels is encoded as a number in the range 0-255, with 0 meaning zero light and 255 meaning maximum light.

Together, there are $256 \times 256 \times 256 = 16.7$ million possible RGB colors which can be displayed by a pixel.

For example, in the setting of RGB (255, 0, 0) it will be displayed as red, because red is set to its highest value (255), and the other two (green and blue) are set to 0.

How Cameras Capture and Store Visual Data

Understanding light behavior is essential to comprehending camera operations. Light moves linearly and is seen by our eyes and cameras as waves. Its characteristics, including variations in wavelength, frequency, and amplitude, are extremely similar to those of sound. Its energy level varies. Cameras function by gathering and capturing light. They consist of two main parts:

1. Lens: Collects light and projects it onto a light detector surface, such as film or a digital sensor. Lenses determine the image projected onto a sensor and are critical in determining the zoom and focus of a given image.

2. Light Detector (Sensor): Converts the captured light into electrical signals. The image sensor contains millions of light-sensitive diodes, or pixels, that collect light and translate it into digital data.

Lens comes into initial contact with the camera. Made up multiple lens groups, lenses decide the image that is projected onto a sensor. It uses some standard formulas like the 50mm f/1.8 or f/1.4 to do so. Focal length will be useful to understand in this context as it is important in determining the zoom of a given image—it is the distance between the point of convergence of lenses and the sensor.

A lens that focuses light onto an image sensor is used by a digital camera to capture a picture. Millions of small light-sensitive diodes, or pixels, make up an image sensor in most cases.

Each photodiode serves as the foundation for light collection, but each sensor also has other components. A semiconductor with a P-N junction makes up the photodiode itself. Electrons are excited when photons strike the photodiode body. A microlens will be placed above each photodiode to focus light on the device's active region. The device has a somewhat wide-band response on its own, so if it is a color sensor, it will typically contain an R, G, or B filter to make it color-sensitive. The lens focuses the light onto the sensor, which converts the light into electrical signals. Thus, the largest voltage we can process should be based on the largest charge we can store.

What happens in low light settings though where the charge collected will be very small in comparison? The analog part of the image processing system usually includes a variable gain amplifier (VGA, also sometimes called a programmable gain amplifier). After that amplifier, there is an analog-to-digital converter. This device processes every pixel's charge-become-voltage and turns that into a 10-bit, 12-bit, 14-bit, or even larger binary numbers. There is also a noise eliminator in order to filter out the dark current.

Cameras apply digital processing to images. They will adjust colors, usually based on a setting such as "Vivid," "Natural," etc. They will analyze the image and apply smoothing algorithms if there is too much noise in the image (low-light shots, generally). They may apply sharpening algorithms as well, sharpening up edges to make the image "pop" and look better than it was. Some may apply a particular film look, or a special "art filter," at the user's option. These processes happen before the image is JPEG encoded, completing the process of image processing.

Modern cameras apply digital processing to images, adjusting colors, smoothing edges, and sharpening details to enhance image quality before encoding them into formats like JPEG. This process involves compressing data to save storage space while retaining essential visual information. The actual storage method used inside the SD card may vary, but one technique uses Flash memory with floating-gate transistors - each bit is stored as a small electric charge on a conductor.

Image formation is a fascinating topic that blends the principles of physics, geometry, and technology. While we've only scratched the surface of this subject, it provides a glimpse into how the field of computer vision leverages these concepts to enable machines to see and interpret the world around them.

3. Introduction to Image Enhancement

As is widely known, Image Enhancement is the process of modifying images so that the important information displayed is more suitable for different processes such as detection and recognition. It involves modifying images to emphasize important information, such as removing noise, sharpening, or adjusting contrast to make key features easier to identify. This chapter explores various techniques used to enhance and filter images in the spatial and frequency domains.

Techniques for Image Enhancement

There are two primary categories of image enhancement techniques:

1. Spatial Domain Techniques: These involve manipulating individual pixels based on their spatial coordinates at a specific resolution. An image can be represented as a 2D matrix where each element represents pixel intensity.

2. Frequency Domain Techniques: These involve transforming the spatial domain of an image into

the frequency domain using methods like the Fourier Transform. This allows the manipulation of pixel groups rather than individual pixels, often used for indirect enhancement.

To understand frequency domain techniques like the Fourier Transform, one must have a grasp of advanced mathematics, but the basic idea is to separate image information into different frequency components.

Common Functions Used in Image Enhancement

Three basic types of functions are frequently used for image enhancement:

1. Linear Functions: Include negative and identity transformations.

2. Logarithmic Functions: Involve log and inverse-log transformations.

3. Power-law Functions: Encompass nth power and nth root transformations.

The negative of an image is produced by subtracting each pixel value from the maximum intensity value, a common technique in enhancing certain image characteristics.

Image Enhancement Algorithms

Several algorithms are used to enhance images, including deblurring, filtering, and contrast adjustment methods. Common techniques for image enhancement are Contrast Stretching, Density Slicing, Edge Enhancement, and Spatial Filtering.

With the advent of AI, new image enhancement tools have been developed, capable of removing blemishes, adding colors, or changing backgrounds by leveraging artificial intelligence algorithms.

We can dive deeper into Spatial Domain Techniques. They can be further divided into:

1. Point Operations (Intensity Transformations): These operations involve applying the same transformation to each pixel in a grayscale image, based on its original pixel value and independent of its location or neighboring pixels.

2. Spatial Filters (or Mask, Kernel): The output value of these operations is dependent on the values of the function $f(x,y)$ and its neighborhood.

3. Frequency Domain: This approach involves enhancing the image by applying a Fourier Transform to the spatial domain, manipulating pixels in groups and indirectly.

As discussed in the previous chapter, we have different types of images like binary, gay-scale, color, and multispectral. Binary images are the simplest type of images and can take on two values, typically black and white, or 0 and 1.

The content analysis of images is accomplished by two primary methods: image processing and pattern recognition. Image processing is a set of computational techniques for analyzing, enhancing, compressing, and reconstructing images.

Applications of Image Enhancement

Here are some practical applications of image enhancement techniques:

Deblurring Images: Helps to improve image clarity.

Contrast Adjustment: Enhances image detail visibility.

Image Brightening: Increases the lightness of an image.

Image Filtering

Image filtering is the process of changing the appearance of an image by altering the colors of the pixels, enhancing contrast, or adding special effects. Filters compensate for image imperfections such as dust particles, noise, interlaced frames, and insufficient sharpness. Filtering is a crucial technique in computer graphics and is often used to emphasize or remove specific features of an image.

Types of Filters

Common types of filters include Median, Minimum, Maximum, Arithmetic Mean, Geometric Mean, and Harmonic Mean filters. These can be used to smooth images, enhance specific details, or compress data.

Smoothing filters help reduce and suppress image noise. Examples include average smoothing, Gaussian smoothing, and adaptive smoothing.

Sharpening filters enhance edges by eliminating blur. These are especially useful in highlighting features and making images more visually striking.

Noise Removal can upgrade image quality and is often introduced during capture, transmission, or processing. Noise removal techniques involve using linear or non-linear filters to decrease noise visibility while maintaining image details. It can be identified in image processing by intensity variance between neighboring pixels.

Grayscale Image Histogram Equalization refers to a transformation where an output image has an approximately uniform distribution of pixels at each gray level. This aids better edge detections and feature extractions.

Image enhancement and filtering are vital in digital image processing, enabling improved visual interpretation, data analysis, and overall image quality. The use of advanced AI-based algorithms further expands the possibilities for refining images and extracting meaningful information from visual data.

4. Introduction to Object Detection and Recognition

Have you ever wondered how computers can look at pictures and figure out what's in them? It's like teaching a computer to see and understand the world around us. Let's explore this fascinating world of object detection, breaking it down into simpler terms.

Object detection and recognition are foundational aspects of computer vision, enabling machines to interpret and understand the visual world. This chapter explores how computers are taught to recognize and categorize objects in images, transforming pixels into meaningful information that can be analyzed, processed, and utilized in various applications, from facial recognition systems to self-driving cars.

The Process of Object Detection

The process of object detection involves identifying and locating objects within an image. This is achieved through several key steps:

Feature Extraction

Finding the Special Parts

Imagine you're trying to recognize your friend's face in a crowded room. You might notice their eyes, nose, and smile. Computers do something similar through a process called feature extraction. It's like teaching the computer to pay attention to special parts, like edges, colors, or textures. This way, the computer learns to recognize important details. The first step in object detection is identifying unique features in an image that can distinguish one object from another. These features may include edges, colors, shapes, or textures.

Object Localization

Where is it?

Now that the computer knows what parts to look for, the next step is figuring out where those parts are in a picture. This is called object localization. It's like telling the computer, "Hey, the face is right here!" This step involves creating bounding boxes around detected objects, helping the system understand their spatial arrangement. Think of it like putting a frame around a picture on your wall. This helps the computer define boundaries and identify what is important and worth focusing on.

Classification Algorithms

Sorting things out

Once the computer knows where the important parts are, it's time to figure out what those parts mean. This is where classification algorithms come in. These are like little decision-makers inside the computer, helping it sort things into categories based on predefined classes such as "cat," "dog," "tree," or "car." For example, if the computer sees a smiling face, it might decide, "Ah, that's a happy person!" The accuracy of these algorithms is crucial for the reliability of the detection system.

Everyday Applications of Object Detection

The ability of machines to detect and recognize objects has transformed many aspects of daily life. Some of the most notable applications include:

Facial Recognition

Facial recognition technology is now everywhere, from unlocking smartphones to enhancing security at airports! This technology works by analyzing unique facial features to verify identity, making it both a convenience and a powerful tool for security. Consider it your own digital bouncer making sure only you get access.

Self-Driving Cars

Imagine cars that can drive themselves! They use object detection to "see" the road. Cameras on these vehicles detect objects such as pedestrians, other cars, and traffic signs, allowing the car to make real-time decisions for safe navigation. It's like having an extra set of eyes to keep everyone safe on the road.

Challenges in Object Detection

Despite significant advancements, object detection technology still faces several challenges. Imagine if you had to find a friend in the dark, it would be tricky, right?

Computers struggle with variability in lighting and occlusion. Object detection systems must contend with varying lighting conditions, occlusions, and partial visibility, which can affect accuracy. These issues require sophisticated algorithms and extensive training data to improve system robustness.

There's also a vast requirement for labeled data to train object detection models, and it's a challenge to find reliable datasets. The quality and diversity of this data directly impact the model's effectiveness and generalizability.

The Future of Object Detection

As technology advances, object detection will become even more sophisticated. Researchers are continuously working to improve detection algorithms, reduce biases, and enhance the accuracy of these systems in complex environments. This progress will lead to broader applications, more reliable systems, and potentially new ways of interacting with technology.

Object detection and recognition represent significant strides in enabling computers to interpret and understand visual data. By breaking down images into recognizable components and categorizing them, machines can make sense of the visual world, paving the way for innovations that could redefine how we live and work.

5. Introduction to Image Segmentation

Image segmentation is a critical process in computer vision that involves dividing a digital image into multiple segments or regions, often referred to as image objects or image regions.

This segmentation process is fundamental for simplifying image representation, making it more meaningful and easier to analyze. By identifying objects and boundaries within images, image segmentation provides the groundwork for advanced image analysis, such as object detection, recognition, and image processing.

The Fundamentals of Image Segmentation

The primary objective of image segmentation is to partition an image into meaningful regions that share similar characteristics, such as color, intensity, or texture. Each pixel in a segmented image is labeled in such a way that pixels with the same labels share specific properties, creating distinct segments that can be analyzed further.

Different neural network implementations and architectures are appropriate for picture segmentation. They often share the same fundamental elements. Two key components of image segmentation are the **encoder** and **decoder**. Encoder refers to a series of layers that extract visual features using deep, focused filters. It learns to recognize specific features based on prior experience, such as object recognition tasks. While an encoder focuses on creating something, a decoder takes its work further. Decoder is a set of layers that transform the output of the encoder into a segmentation mask corresponding to the pixel resolution of the input image.

These components work together, often incorporating skip connections—long-range connections within a neural network that allow the model to recognize features at different scales, improving segmentation accuracy.

Types of Image Segmentation

There are several approaches to image segmentation, each serving different purposes and applications:

1. Semantic Segmentation: In semantic segmentation, every pixel in an image is assigned to a class based on its semantic meaning. There is no differentiation between individual objects as it groups objects by type—there is no reference to any other context or data. For example, in an image containing multiple

trees and vehicles, all trees might be categorized under a single "tree" class, while all vehicles (cars, buses, bicycles) fall under a "vehicle" class.

2. Instance Segmentation: Unlike semantic segmentation, instance segmentation differentiates between distinct instances of an item. This is ideal for scenarios where specific object identification is required as it divides overlapping regions based on object boundaries. For example, in a busy street scene, instance segmentation would identify each person separately rather than grouping them all under the "person" category. This approach is essential in scenarios where object counting or specific object identification is required.

3. Panoptic Segmentation: This is a more recent development in image segmentation. It is a more comprehensive method that combines semantic and instance segmentation. It distinguishes between each occurrence of objects by assigning unique labels while also categorizing them based on semantic identification. In cases where a lot of information is needed to function, panoptic segmentation proves to be useful. For example, self-driving cars need precision and they must be able to comprehend their environment swiftly. Panoptic segmentation is

helpful for them as it can segment a live stream of pictures.

Thresholding Techniques for Segmentation

Thresholding is one of the most straightforward techniques for image segmentation, involving the conversion of grayscale images into binary images based on a specified threshold value. Comparing each pixel's intensity with a predetermined value (threshold) separates the pixels in a picture. Pixels are classified as either foreground or background, depending on whether their intensity is above or below this threshold.

Interestingly, the threshold value (T) is not constant, as it only works if the image includes very little noise. Several thresholding methods are categorized differently based on various threshold values:

1. Simple Thresholding: With this technique, one can replace pixel values with black or white, depending on whether they fall below or exceed a fixed threshold. If the value is higher than the threshold, you replace a pixel with white. If it's lower, you swap it with black! This basic method is suitable for images with minimal noise and a good start for novice users.

2. Otsu's Binarization: In straightforward thresholding, picture segmentation was

accomplished by selecting a fixed threshold value. But how can you tell if the value you chose was the appropriate one? Testing many values and selecting one is a simple solution, but it is not the most effective one. Consider a photo that has a histogram with two peaks—one for the foreground and one for the background—in the image. The approximate value of the midpoint of those peaks may be used as your threshold value when employing Otsu binarization. This method is particularly effective for bimodal images, where two distinct peaks represent foreground and background. This method is often used to scan documents, identify patterns, and eliminate extraneous colors from a file.

3. Adaptive Thresholding: For every image, it might not be appropriate to use the same threshold setting as different backdrops and circumstances have an impact on the qualities of various photos. As a result, you may keep the threshold value flexible rather than employing a single fixed threshold value to conduct segmentation on the whole picture. Instead of using a single global threshold, adaptive thresholding adjusts the threshold dynamically for different regions of an image, accommodating variations in lighting and contrast. This technique is particularly useful for images with uneven lighting conditions.

Edge-Based Segmentation

One of the most widely used processes used in image segmentation is edge-based segmentation. It focuses on detecting the boundaries of objects within an image by identifying discontinuities in intensity or color. It is an essential step as it enables one to identify the characteristics of the various items in the image. This method leverages algorithms to detect edges based on changes in texture, contrast, and other attributes. It makes it easy for users to remove extraneous and superfluous information from an image. It greatly decreases the size of the image, which facilitates analysis of the same.

There are many edge-based segmentation methods available. We can divide them into two categories:

Search-Based Edge Detection

Search-based edge detection methods focus on computing a measure of edge strength and look for local directional maxima of the gradient magnitude through a computed estimate of the edge's local orientation.

Zero-Crossing Based Edge Detection

Zero-crossing-based edge detection methods look for zero crossings in a derivative expression retrieved from the image to find the edges.

Typically, one has to pre-process the image to remove unwanted noise and make it easier to detect edges. Canny, Prewitt, Deriche, and Roberts Cross are some of the most popular edge detection operators for the same purpose. They make it easier to detect discontinuities and find the edges.

In edge-based detection, your goal is to get a partial segmentation minimum where you can group all the local edges into a binary image. In your newly created binary image, the edge chains must match the existing components of the image in question.

Clustering-Based Segmentation Algorithms

Clustering algorithms are unsupervised techniques that group pixels with similar characteristics into clusters, providing another powerful approach to image segmentation. These algorithms help reveal hidden patterns and structures that may not be immediately apparent. Key clustering techniques include:

K-means Clustering: A simple and widely used algorithm that divides an image into a predefined number of clusters based on pixel similarity.

Fuzzy C-means Clustering: An extension of K-means where pixels can belong to multiple clusters with varying degrees of membership, providing a more flexible segmentation.

Image segmentation is a vital process in computer vision, providing the foundation for understanding and analyzing complex visual data. By breaking down images into meaningful regions, segmentation techniques enable a wide range of applications, from medical imaging to autonomous vehicles, facilitating a deeper understanding of the visual world.

6. Introduction to Optical Character Recognition (OCR)

Optical Character Recognition (OCR) is a transformative technology that converts images of text into machine-readable formats. As a foundational tool in the digitization of text, OCR bridges the gap between the physical and digital worlds, enabling computers to recognize and process printed or handwritten text from documents, images, and other sources. Have you scanned a receipt on your phone and been amazed at the ability of your phone to read it accurately? That is because of OCR. This chapter provides an overview of OCR, its evolution, underlying techniques, and practical applications.

The Evolution of OCR Technology

The origins of OCR technology can be traced back to early innovations in telegraphy and reading devices for the visually impaired. In 1914, Emanuel Goldberg developed a machine that read characters and converted them into standard telegraph code, marking the beginning of OCR development. Concurrently, Edmund Fournier d'Albe developed the Optophone, a device that produced tones corresponding to printed letters when scanned across a page.

By the late 1920s and 1930s, OCR technology evolved further with Goldberg's invention of the "Statistical Machine" for searching microfilm archives using an optical code recognition system, leading to the first OCR-related patent acquired by IBM. Since then, OCR has grown from a niche technology to a widely used tool in various industries, powered by advances in machine learning and neural networks.

How OCR Works

Optical character recognition (OCR) is sometimes referred to as text recognition. An OCR program extracts and repurposes data from scanned documents, camera images and image-only pdf files.

OCR involves several steps to convert text images into machine-readable formats. Key stages in the OCR process include preprocessing, character segmentation, character recognition, and post-processing. Various businesses use OCR as an efficiency tool as it can be useful in different scenarios. For example, it scans and reads number plates and road signs in self-driving cars, detects brand logos in social media posts, or identifies product packaging in advertising images.

OCR engine uses algorithms such as Convolutional Neural Networks (CNNs), Support Vector Machines (SVMs), or Hidden Markov Models (HMMs) to identify and classify the characters. Modern OCR systems can recognize a wide range of fonts, styles, and languages, enabling them to handle diverse document types.

Techniques of OCR

There are various techniques involved in OCR.

1. *De-skew* - Deskewing is a process whereby skew is removed by rotating an image by the same amount as its skew but in the opposite direction. This results in a horizontally and vertically aligned image where the text runs across the page rather than at an angle.

2. *Despeckle* – It is the technique, involving the removal of, any digital image spots or smoothing the edges of text images.

3. *Binarization* – This technique involves converting a colored image into an image that consists of only black and white pixels.

4. *Line Removal* – This technique involves removal of horizontal or vertical lines that run through text and which can interfere with optical character recognition.

5. *Zoning* – This involves creating zones in documents and setting specific margins for entire pages. Data is then extracted from these specified areas while anything cropped out is left out of processing.

6. *Line and Word Detection* – OCR Line Detection algorithms are able to accurately identify and extract the text from each individual line of an image, allowing you to easily extract and process the information contained within the document

7. *Script Recognition* – Technique uses readability to identify script entered.

8. *Character Isolation or "Segmentation"* – For per-character OCR, multiple characters that are connected due to image artifacts must be separated; single characters that are broken into multiple pieces due to artifacts must be connected.

Challenges in OCR

Despite its effectiveness, OCR technology faces several challenges. One of the main struggles is dealing with diverse text formats and languages. Text can appear in various languages, scripts, fonts, and orientations, complicating recognition. OCR systems must be trained extensively to handle these variations.

There are also issues of extracting data related to cost and time while maintaining accuracy. Low-resolution images, distorted text, or images with noise and blurring present significant hurdles for OCR systems, requiring advanced preprocessing techniques to mitigate these issues.

OCR technology is limited to text recognition and is not able to recognize or extract other types of data such as images or graphics. This can be problematic for businesses and organizations that have to process documents that contain a combination of text and other types of data. Recognizing handwritten text is particularly challenging due to the variability in handwriting styles and quality, making it harder for OCR engines to accurately interpret and process.

Many OCR engines fail to support and understand the complexity of the input data in a given document. For example, if the input document is a form then the OCR might identify the text but may not recognize text over a line or, the text in blocks. This may result in unexpected output.

Applications of OCR

OCR technology has a wide range of practical applications across industries, transforming how businesses, institutions, and individuals manage information. Key applications include:

Document Digitization

OCR is widely used to convert printed documents, such as books, invoices, and contracts, into digital formats, making them searchable and easy to store.

Automatic Number Plate Recognition (ANPR)

In transportation and law enforcement, OCR helps identify vehicle number plates for traffic monitoring and enforcement.

Assistive Technology for the Visually Impaired

OCR is employed in assistive devices that read printed text aloud, providing access to printed information for those with visual impairments.

Business Card Scanning

OCR is used to convert information from business cards into digital contact lists, enhancing productivity and organization.

Form Processing

OCR technology enables automated data entry by extracting information from forms, surveys, and questionnaires, reducing manual labor and errors.

The Future of OCR

As OCR technology continues to evolve, advancements in deep learning and artificial intelligence will lead to even more robust and versatile OCR systems. Future developments will likely focus on improving the recognition of handwritten text, supporting more complex document layouts, and integrating OCR with other AI technologies for broader applications.

OCR has become an integral part of the digital world, enabling seamless conversion of text from physical to digital formats. As technology continues to advance, OCR will remain a crucial tool for data processing, information retrieval, and enhancing accessibility, driving innovation across various sectors.

7. Introduction to Augmented Reality (AR)

Augmented Reality (AR) represents an innovative technology that blends the digital and physical worlds, overlaying computer-generated content onto real-world environments. Unlike Virtual Reality (VR), which immerses users in a completely artificial environment,

AR enhances the real world by adding digital elements that interact seamlessly with what we see, hear, and feel. This chapter explores the technologies behind AR, its applications, and the challenges and future directions of this rapidly evolving field.

Understanding Augmented Reality: Where Real and Virtual Coexist

At its core, AR serves as a bridge between the tangible and virtual realms, enriching everyday experiences with additional layers of information. Like a digital magician, it enriches our daily experiences. By superimposing digital images, sounds, or data onto the real world, AR offers a unique and interactive experience that transforms how users perceive their surroundings. This is achieved through devices such as smartphones, tablets, or specialized AR glasses, which process and project digital content in real time.

An interesting example of AR is the E.D.I.T.H. glasses featured in *Spider-Man: No Way Home*. These glasses use computer vision techniques to analyze the environment, highlight objects, and project relevant information directly onto the user's retinas, showcasing a futuristic vision of AR technology.

The Technologies Behind Augmented Reality: Magic Unveiled

AR technology relies on several key components to function effectively:

Marker-Based Tracking

Imagine you hold up your phone, and, as if by magic, additional information appears on the screen when the camera detects a specific object or image. This is marker-based AR. This method uses specific visual markers, such as QR codes or predefined images, to trigger the display of digital content. When a device's camera detects a marker, it overlays relevant information on the screen. It's like a secret code that unlocks a virtual treasure.

Markerless Tracking

Now, picture AR that doesn't rely on markers but understands your surroundings naturally. Unlike marker-based tracking, markerless AR uses sensors, GPS, and visual recognition to understand the environment and accurately place digital content in real-world contexts. This technology enables digital elements to appear seamlessly integrated into the surroundings without the need for predefined markers.

Real-World Applications of Augmented Reality: Bringing it to Life

The practical applications of AR span across numerous fields, offering new ways to interact with information and the environment:

Gaming and Entertainment: Games like *Pokémon GO* have revolutionized mobile gaming by using AR to place virtual characters within the player's real-world environment, merging physical exploration with digital interaction. Through AR, Pikachu and his friends appear next to you!

Interactive Education: AR has transformed educational experiences by making learning more interactive. Imagine studying Biology and you see a 3D model of a cell hovering above your textbook! There are endless possibilities of enhancing comprehension through hands-on engagement.

Navigation and Wayfinding: AR-based navigation apps overlay directions, street names, and points of interest onto the real world as seen through a smartphone or AR glasses, reducing the likelihood of getting lost and making navigation more intuitive.

Retail and E-Commerce: Ever wanted to try on clothes without actually changing? AR lets you do just that. AR enables virtual try-ons, allowing users to see how clothes, accessories, or even furniture will look on them or in their homes before making a purchase, enhancing customer satisfaction and reducing return rates.

Medical Training and Simulations: In the healthcare sector, AR provides valuable training tools for medical professionals, enabling them to practice procedures on virtual patients overlaid in real environments, enhancing their skills without risk.

Challenges in Augmented Reality: The AR Adventure Continues

While AR offers exciting opportunities, it also presents several technical and ethical challenges. There are technical issues of ensuring the seamless integration of virtual and real-world elements that require precise tracking, robust hardware, and advanced algorithms. Improving these aspects remains a key challenge for developers. There are also privacy concerns. As AR devices continuously capture and process real-world data, there are concerns about how this data is stored, shared, and used. Addressing privacy and security issues is essential for the widespread adoption of AR technology.

The Future of Augmented Reality

The future of AR is promising, with continuous advancements in technology expected to lead to more sophisticated and accessible experiences. Innovations in artificial intelligence, machine learning, and hardware miniaturization will enhance AR capabilities, making devices more powerful and user-friendly. As these technologies evolve, AR is poised to become an integral part of daily life, offering new dimensions to how we work, learn, play, and connect with the world around us.

Augmented Reality stands at the forefront of technological innovation, transforming how we interact with our environment by seamlessly blending the digital with the physical. As AR technology continues to advance, it will open up new possibilities across various sectors, from entertainment and education to healthcare and commerce, reshaping our perception of what is real and what is possible. It's the digital fairy godmother that transforms the mundane into the magical, showing us that the boundaries between what's real and what's virtual are wonderfully fluid.

8. Demystifying Deep Learning and Neural Networks

In the enchanting world of technology, there's a type of wizardry known as Deep Learning and Neural Networks. These are not just buzzwords; they're the secret sauce behind some of the most incredible advancements, especially in computer vision. Deep learning and neural networks are at the core of modern artificial intelligence, driving advancements in fields ranging from computer vision to natural language processing. This chapter explores the fundamental concepts behind deep learning and neural networks, unraveling the complexities of these technologies and their transformative impact.

The ABCs of Deep Learning: Getting Started

At the heart of deep learning is the concept of neural networks, computational models inspired by the human brain's structure and function. Imagine a neural network as a team of tiny wizards, each responsible for recognizing different aspects of a problem.

Neurons: The Building Blocks of Neural Networks and Tiny Wizards

Neurons in a neural network are the fundamental units that process data. These wizards work together to solve a problem. Each neuron processes a small piece of information and passes it along.

Layers: Building the Magical Tower

Neurons are organized in layers, creating a tower of magical processing. The first layer gets the raw data, like pixels from an image. Each subsequent layer refines the information until the final layer produces an answer or a prediction.

The depth of a neural network—defined by the number of hidden layers—determines its capacity to learn complex patterns. Deeper networks can capture more intricate relationships in the data but require more computational power and training data.

Deep vs. Shallow Learning: The Depth Matters

When we say "deep" learning, it means we have many layers in our tower of neurons. The depth allows the network to understand complex patterns and relationships in data, making it a powerful problem-solving tool.

Neural Networks in Action: Solving Puzzles with Computer Vision

Now, let's talk about computer vision – the wizardry that lets computers see and understand the visual world. Neural Networks are like the Sherlock Holmes of computer vision, solving mysteries hidden in images and videos.

Image Recognition: Identifying Faces and More

Think of a neural network as a detective looking at a photo. The first layer might notice edges and colors, the next one puts together shapes, and the final layers recognize complex objects like faces or cars. This is how your phone recognizes your friend's face in a photo.

Object Detection: Spotting Multiple Things

Sometimes, the detective needs to find multiple things in one image. Object detection is like the detective pointing at each item, saying, "There's a cat, a chair, and a plant!" Neural Networks can do this lightning-fast, even in a crowd of objects.

Semantic Segmentation: Understanding Boundaries

Imagine coloring a picture – staying within the lines. Neural Networks can do that too! They understand the boundaries of different objects in an image, separating the sky from the sea or the road from the sidewalk.

Image Generation: Creating New Magic

Neural Networks can even generate new images. It's like having a painting wizard. Show it some examples, and it can create entirely new artworks or even realistic faces that never existed.

The Complexity Challenge: Cracking Hard Nuts

Now, let's talk about the challenge. These networks can get big, with millions of neurons and complex connections. Training them – teaching them the magic – can be a bit like teaching a dragon. It requires tons of data, powerful computers, and lots of patience.

Data: The Spell Book for Learning

Neural Networks need examples to learn. For image recognition, they need thousands of images to understand what a cat looks like from different angles, in various lighting conditions, and amidst different backgrounds.

Computational Power: Wizards Need Muscle

Training these networks is like performing a magical ritual. It demands powerful computers with graphical processing units (GPUs) that can handle the heavy lifting of all those calculations.

Complex Problems: The Ultimate Quests

Deep Learning and Neural Networks thrive on solving complex puzzles. Whether it's diagnosing diseases from medical images, understanding human emotions from facial expressions, or even helping cars navigate autonomously – these are the ultimate quests for our digital wizards.

Applications of Neural Networks in Computer Vision

Neural networks have revolutionized computer vision, enabling machines to interpret and understand visual data in unprecedented ways. Key applications include image recognition, object detection, semantic segmentation, and image generation.

Neural networks can identify objects, faces, and scenes in images by analyzing pixel patterns. This technology powers applications like photo tagging on social media and facial recognition in security systems. Beyond recognizing single objects, neural networks can detect and locate multiple objects within an image. This capability is crucial for self-driving cars, which must identify pedestrians, vehicles, and traffic signs in real time. Neural networks can also generate new images from scratch, creating realistic faces, landscapes, or even artwork. This capability is powered by models such as Generative Adversarial Networks (GANs), which learn to create high-quality images by pitting two networks against each other.

The Future of Deep Learning

The future of deep learning lies in addressing these challenges and extending its capabilities to new domains. Researchers are working on developing more efficient algorithms that require less data and computational power, making deep learning accessible to a broader audience. Advances in transfer learning, unsupervised learning, and reinforcement learning are opening new avenues for neural networks to learn from fewer examples and adapt to new tasks.

Deep learning and neural networks are revolutionizing the way machines understand and interact with the world. By mimicking the human brain's ability to learn from experience, these technologies are driving innovations across industries, from healthcare to autonomous vehicles. As research progresses, deep learning will continue to push the boundaries of what is possible, offering new insights and solutions to some of the most complex problems of our time.

9. Navigating Ethics in Computer Vision— A Compass for Transparent and Responsible Use

As computer vision technologies continue to advance, they open up new vistas of possibilities for innovation across fields such as healthcare, security, transportation, and more. However, with these advancements comes the responsibility to consider the ethical implications of these technologies. This chapter explores the ethical dimensions of computer vision, emphasizing the need for transparency, fairness, and accountability in the development and deployment of these systems.

The Power and Responsibility of Sight: Why Ethics Matter

From ChatGPT to iPhones, technology is rooted in ethical use. Every product is built on ethical rules and accountability systems. Computer vision systems can interpret and analyze vast amounts of visual data, which can include personal and sensitive information. As these systems become increasingly integrated into everyday life, ethical considerations are essential to ensure that the technology is used responsibly and does not infringe on individual rights.

Key ethical concerns in computer vision include:

Privacy and Surveillance

Computer vision often involves the collection and analysis of images and videos, which may contain personal information. Without proper safeguards, this data can be misused for invasive surveillance or unauthorized monitoring, raising significant privacy concerns.

Bias and Fairness

If the data used to train computer vision models is biased, the systems may produce biased results, leading to unfair outcomes. For example, facial recognition systems have been shown to have higher error rates for certain demographic groups, potentially leading to discrimination.

Transparency and Accountability

Understanding how computer vision systems work should not be shrouded in mystery. Ethical use requires transparency, where users, developers, and those impacted by these technologies can comprehend how decisions are made.

Security Risks

In the wrong hands, computer vision technology could be exploited for malicious purposes, such as creating deepfakes or conducting unauthorized surveillance. Ethical considerations must include implementing safeguards to prevent misuse and protect against security threats.

Guiding Principles for Ethical Computer Vision

To address these concerns, several guiding principles can help ensure ethical practices in computer vision:

Inclusive Data Collection

To avoid biases, data used to train computer vision models must be diverse and representative of different demographics, cultures, and environments. This helps to prevent the technology from favoring one group over another and ensures more equitable outcomes.

Bias Detection and Mitigation

Regular audits of computer vision systems are necessary to identify and correct biases. When biases are detected, steps should be taken to adjust the models and improve fairness. Transparency in this process is essential for maintaining public trust.

Privacy by Design

Ethical considerations must be prioritized from the very beginning of system design. Implementing privacy-preserving techniques, such as anonymization and encryption, helps protect individuals' personal information from misuse.

Explainability and Interpretability:

Users and stakeholders should be able to understand how computer vision systems arrive at their decisions. Providing explanations and insights into the decision-making processes enhances accountability and builds trust between technology providers and users.

Consent and Communication

Users should be fully informed about how computer vision technologies may impact them and should have the option to provide or withhold consent. Ethical practices involve clear communication of the technology's purpose and capabilities, as well as the ability to opt-out when desired.

Continuous Evaluation and Improvement

Ethical responsibility extends beyond the initial development phase. Regular evaluations of computer vision systems should be conducted to identify areas for improvement and address emerging ethical concerns. This proactive approach ensures that the technology remains aligned with societal values and expectations.

Real-World Applications and Ethical Considerations

The ethical implications of computer vision are particularly evident in specific real-world applications:

Facial Recognition Technology: The use of facial recognition in public spaces has sparked debate due to concerns over privacy and potential misuse of surveillance. Issues such as accuracy discrepancies across demographics and potential discrimination highlight the need for stringent ethical guidelines and oversight.

Autonomous Vehicles: As autonomous vehicles become more prevalent, ethical considerations come into play. Ensuring the safety of passengers and pedestrians, addressing biases in object recognition, and establishing accountability in case of accidents are critical ethical challenges.

Medical Imaging and Diagnostics: In the realm of medical imaging, ethical considerations involve safeguarding patient privacy, ensuring the accuracy of diagnoses, and transparently communicating the limitations of the technology to healthcare professionals.

The Path Forward: Striking an Ethical Balance

Navigating the ethical landscape of computer vision requires a balanced approach that promotes innovation while protecting individual rights and societal values. As these technologies become more widespread, developers, policymakers, and stakeholders must engage in ongoing dialogue, collaboration, and ethical evaluation.

Ethics should not be seen as a hindrance but as a guiding framework that ensures technology works for the benefit of all, upholding integrity and public trust. The ethical considerations discussed in this chapter serve as a compass for navigating the challenges and opportunities that lie ahead in the field of computer vision.

Ethical considerations are fundamental to the responsible development and deployment of computer vision technologies. By prioritizing transparency, fairness, privacy, and accountability, we can harness the full potential of computer vision to improve lives while safeguarding our values and rights. As technology evolves, so too must our commitment to ethical principles, ensuring that progress is made with respect for all.